Your Re-entry Path: Restore
Help for the Transition Season

Shonna Ingram

All rights reserved. No part of this book may be used or reproduced in any manner without written permission from the author and publisher. This work is solely for personal growth and education. It should not be treated as a substitute for professional assistance, therapeutic activities such as psychotherapy or counseling, or medical advice. In the event of physical or mental distress, please consult with appropriate health professionals, and in an extreme case, the emergency room of your local hospital. The application of protocols and information in this book is the choice of each reader, who assumes full responsibility for his or her understanding, interpretation, and results. The author and publisher assume no responsibility for the actions or choices of any reader.

Scripture quotations marked NIV are taken from HOLY BIBLE, NEW INTERNATIONAL VERSION.
Copyright © 1973, 1978, 1984 by International Bible Society. Used by permission of Zondervan Publishing House. All rights reserved.

Scripture quotations marked ESV are taken from The Holy Bible, English Standard Version (ESV). Copyright © 2001 by Crossway, a publishing ministry of Good News Publishers. Used by permission. All rights reserved.

Cover image *Canva Blue and Brown Photography Journey of Life Ebook cover by Notisnal Studio*

Copyright © 2022 Shonna Ingram
shonnaingram.com
All rights reserved.
ISBN: 978-1-7370661-4-9

DEDICATION

To those in a season of unclarity and transition as they find their next path.

Contents

Introduction to the Re-entry Path Series

Week 1- **Stepping onto the Path**

Week 2 - **Living with Loss: A Perspective Shift**

Week 3 - **The Practice of Lament: Our Heart's Cry**

Week 4 - **Self-Forgiveness: Forgiveness or Release**

Week 5 - **Forgiving Others: Covenant Promise**

Week 6 - **Reflection and Review**

Appendix

References

Recommended Resources

Introduction to the Re-entry Path Series

Re-entry can be one of the most difficult seasons in the life of a missionary worker. At least that was my experience. I began my ministry journey over 20 years ago as a pastor's wife, and after a few years, we transitioned to mission work in Africa, where we helped start 15 New Testament translation projects. When it was time to return from the field, we felt a clear leading from God to do so. We made a plan and ended our overseas work as well as we could.

I thought I knew what I was getting into as I returned to my home country. I was wrong! Returning to America became one of the hardest seasons of my life. We hadn't had an opportunity to process what happened to us on the field, we lost our biggest supporting church a few months after returning, we weren't sure what our new roles would be, and the kids had a difficult time adjusting. We felt so alone.

During that transition season, the emotional storm that had started brewing during our last term overseas released a pile of carnage in its path. The stress affected my physical health, and my emotional and spiritual health suffered. My husband and I experienced marriage issues for the first time in over 20 years. It felt like we were sinking fast, and we had no clarity on how to move forward. I became angry, depressed, and full of anxiety. God wasn't showing up, at least not in the same way He had before, and He sure wasn't making it easy to believe that He was both good and all-powerful.

I specifically remember sitting in my room a few months in, thinking that we had given up everything to move our family of six overseas, and this was what we got in return? I had no one to guide me through this season who understood my pain.

I started talking with a few other couples who had returned to the States around the same time we had. They were feeling the same way we were: stuck and unsure of how to move forward on the journey. This made me think that there had to be a better way to support people in re-entry.

Then God took me on a journey. First, I had an opportunity to learn about coaching. Coaching was just coming onto the missions scene in 2013 when we returned. The idea behind coaching is to help people get unstuck and start to move forward. I knew I needed to get unstuck, but there were still too many missing pieces in my life to be able to make a plan and move forward.

Six months later, my director said the missionary care team (did I mention I was on the missionary care team through all of this?) was going to take a Trauma Healing training course. I thought that sounded like a good idea because I was sure some of our missionaries had experienced trauma — or would in the future. During that training, God met me in the dark places of my soul for the first time in a very long time. I learned what trauma really was, I realized that I was experiencing trauma, and I recognized that this was why I hadn't been able to move forward, in spite of the coaching. In this training, I also learned the tools I needed to begin processing the trauma.

A few months later I had the opportunity to become a career guidance advisor. During this training, I learned the unique way God had created me. I discovered where I was in my current life season, and I had the opportunity to create my next purpose after having lost my identity as a cross-cultural worker. I began to set healthy boundaries so I could serve others out of a full cup instead of an empty one.

Throughout this process, I began noticing that there were many books on coaching, many books on trauma, and many books on career development, but I hadn't seen one resource that combined all three methodologies. This observation led me to write a trauma recovery series entitled *Your Path to Renewed Hope*.

A few years into using that material with clients, I noticed some common themes from people transitioning through re-entry. They were questioning their vocational path, grappling with the loss of their identity, losing strong connections with friends and family, wondering where they fit into their local church, and even questioning what they believed. I watched people who could have been helped during the re-entry process but who ended up leaving missions – and some even left their faith altogether. This grieves me more than anything because this season can be one of the best growth opportunities.

So I decided to adapt my *Renewed Hope* series for missionaries going through re-entry. And that is what you hold in your hands today: the first of three workbooks in *Your Re-entry Path*.

It has been a great joy to share these tools with people. It is a privilege to watch God show up for my clients the way He showed up for me. I have seen people find hope and step into something new. I have seen people get job offers out of the blue. I see how they set safe, healthy boundaries, and I have even seen physical and emotional healing. But more than anything, I have seen people experience Jesus as their healer and form a stronger relationship with Him.

I was able to take the hardest season of my life and turn it into something meaningful and beautiful. This is why I'm so passionate about serving returning missionaries. And over the last several years, I've had the privilege of helping people walk through the re-entry process. Now I get to share these resources with a wider audience.

I believe that mission organizations need more education on re-entry and that missionaries need more structures in place to help in this difficult season. Most of my mission training was focused on getting us overseas and keeping us there. However, the latest statistics show that many people are only staying on the field for five to seven years, and Covid didn't help this situation. That makes this education critical to the future of missions.

A Roadmap for the Re-entry Path

This series is divided into two workbooks, each of which will guide you through a different season of re-entry. You will begin with *Restore,* and when you are ready, you can move on to *Rebuild*.

Restore

Restore helps you start the healing process. You will learn trauma principles, check in with yourself, and spend time processing the past. You will gain tools for processing your grief and loss through the practice of lament, and you will learn about forgiveness and how to do it from a place of rest.

Rebuild

Rebuild gives you the opportunity to heal from a place of being intimately known and continuously restored. You will start by using career and self-development principles to pause and receive insight from God. You will discover what you can bring to the world. Then in a few weeks, you will apply post-traumatic growth and coaching principles so you can implement what you've learned to live life with God in your next season.

My prayer is not only for your healing and growth in your re-entry season but also for your next hard season – for there will be others. May the tools you receive in this series prepare you to approach trials with wisdom and grace, and may they bring you ever closer to Jesus.

Overview of how we are going to spend our time

This series is split into two workbooks which each contain six chapters. Each chapter contains a week's worth of material spread out over five days. However, some exercises may take more than a day to process.

You should pay attention to what is happening inside you and feel free to go back and do a week over if needed – or even repeat a week several times. I like to tell people that this isn't a "one-and-done" study and that you might not finish it within the suggested timeline. If you want to stick more closely to the suggested six-week timeline, I suggest enlisting a friend or coach to help you stay on track. You could also join one of our six-week groups.

In the first week of *Restore*, you will look at where you currently are in your Body, Heart, and Soul. If at any time you need extra processing pages, you'll be able to download them from the website.

Before we start Week 1, we will meet Elizabeth, a client who started her journey where you are right now. As you work through the book, you will see how she walks through her own re-entry season.

Let's Meet Elizabeth

Elizabeth grew up in a Christian home and felt the "call to ministry" in high school during a short-term mission trip. After college, she joined a mission organization and moved overseas. The time she spent overseas was hard, but she had expected that. Several years later, she unexpectedly returned to the U.S. because of an illness her doctors couldn't diagnose. She was emotionally and physically drained. She felt stuck; she had lost her identity and any hope for the future.

Elizabeth entered a major life transition. She was confused because there wasn't one catastrophic event that caused all her unclarity. All she knew was that the way she felt about herself, the world, and God was different than it had been before, and she didn't know where to go next. She started questioning. "Where is Jesus in this season?" "Who am I now?" "How do I move forward?" She was overwhelmed and confused. She knew there had to be a better way, but she didn't know how to move forward.

After a few conversations with Elizabeth, I knew where she needed to start. Even though she did not feel ready to begin, I knew she was.

Overall, we spent a year together creating something new for her. It wasn't always easy, but she stuck it out, and by the end of that year, she knew her next purpose and how to continue to move forward. Most of all she had hope – a hope that she had never felt before.

There are a lot of Elizabeths out there floundering around trying to figure out their re-entry path on their own. I know because I was one of them.

Reflection

What thoughts and feelings come to mind, so far?

_____
_____
_____
_____
_____
_____
_____
_____
_____
_____
_____
_____
_____

Reminder During Restore

You might have more than one Restore season.

Your time in *Restore* can be the hardest and longest season — it is ok if it takes you longer than the suggested amount of time.

Jesus is here — even when you can't feel Him and you don't know what He is doing.

You might need medication — if a doctor recommends an antidepressant or some other medication during this time, take your medication. It is a part of your healing process.

Week 1- *Stepping onto the Path*

Getting Ready for Week 1

This week you will start the *Restore* process, the first step on your Re-entry Path. We need to start where you currently are. First, you will create your declaration verse that you will use throughout your time in *Restore*. It will help you rest in the Lord. Then you will create safety for your body (including your mind and brain), your heart, and your soul.

As you start, I ask that you be honest with yourself so you can notice if anything needs to change, no matter how big or small.

Day 1 - Creating Your Declaration Verse

Day 2 - Where are you on your Re-entry Path?

Day 3 - Nourish your Body, Heart, and Soul

Day 4 - Building Safety

Day 5 - End of Week Reflection

Day 1
Creating Your Declaration Verse

Sometimes, returning to our passport country leads us to question where God is and what is happening around us. As believers, this might be an uncomfortable season, and we might feel guilty about asking questions that we once thought we had the answers to. We need to give ourselves permission to spend some time here.

Depending on how you experienced overseas life and whether you've already participated in other debriefings, this part of the journey might feel short and easy, or it might feel long and difficult. Both of these experiences are normal, and you're not alone if you happen to be in a season of prolonged unclarity.

During this time the most important thing we can do is enter into a season of rest in God. The Bible is full of examples of people resting in God. David, Elijah, and Paul are just a few examples.

There are many passages of scripture that talk about a season of rest. I want to focus on a familiar passage.

Psalm 23, especially verse 3. (ESV)

1 The Lord is my shepherd; I shall not want.
2 He makes me lie down in green pastures. He leads me beside still waters.
3 **He restores my soul. He** leads me in paths of righteousness for **his name's sake.**
4 Even though I walk through the valley of the shadow of death, I will fear no evil, for you are with me; your rod and your staff, they comfort me.

During my research of this verse, I learned that the use of the word **Restore** in this passage indicates **something being done continuously.**

This means the Shepherd is **"continuously restoring."** What does "continuously restoring" mean to you?

_____
_____
_____
_____
_____

Read through the verse again. Why is He restoring us?

_____
_____

For His Name, so He can be glorified.
You might not feel like you are in a season where He can be glorified in you. I understand that feeling! Stay with the passage a little longer.

Read through these verses again. Who restores our soul?
_____
_____

He does! He is the one leading this process. We get to receive what He has already done for us.

What would receiving continuous restoration look like for you?
_____
_____
_____
_____
_____

Introducing the Biblical Practice for *Restore*

The biblical practice is simple: at the end of each day, speak *Psalm 23:1-4 out loud.* Sometimes it can be helpful to write scripture in our own words. There is space below for you to rewrite Psalm 23:1-4 in your own words. Later you can choose to recite your own version of Psalm 23 or another version.
_____
_____
_____
_____
_____

This practice allows us to enter into that season of rest and see what He is doing in and around us. It also reminds us that we are in a season of expectation, of waiting to see what the Lord will do.

At the end of each day, you will see a statement that says:
"End today by remembering your Declaration Verse."

Reflection

Take some time to share your thoughts about entering into a season of rest in God.

_____
_____
_____
_____
_____
_____
_____
_____
_____
_____
_____
_____
_____
_____
_____
_____
_____
_____
_____
_____
_____
_____
_____
_____
_____
_____
_____
_____
_____

Extra activity: In the space below, draw a picture of you sitting by the still waters.

Day 2
Where are you on your Re-entry Path?

Today, we are going to start the process of focusing on where you are in your re-entry. There isn't a perfect return, and there isn't always a clear next step, but there are things we can choose to do.

Was your re-entry expected or unexpected?
_____

How long has it been since you returned?
_____
_____

Where do you consider yourself to be on your re-entry path? (You could be at the beginning, middle, or end, or you may have no idea.)

_____
_____
_____
_____

What feelings and emotions come up when you think about the re-entry process so far?

What has been the hardest part?
___

What has been the best part?
___

What resources have gotten you this far?
___

End today by remembering your Declaration Verse.
*If very negative emotions surface, please connect with someone that you trust to talk about it.

Day 3
Nourish Your Body, Heart, and Soul

I chose the word "nourish" because it means *to cause to grow or live in a healthy state*. To do that we will be focusing on our Body, Heart, and Soul. They all give us important information about what is going on inside us, and we need to listen to each one, especially in this season of Rest.

We will be looking at how to:
Nourish your Body through Sleep, Nutrition, and Physical Movement
Nourish your Heart through Input
Nourish your Soul through Prayer and Rest

Nourish Your Body

I use the term "Body" not only to mean your physical body, but also your brain and mind. You nourish all of them the same way through Sleep, Nutrition, and Physical Movement.

How is your sleep?
On average how many hours of sleep do you get per night?
_____

How restful has your sleep been lately?
_____
_____

Are you getting up in the middle of the night because of kids, bladder problems, medication, or insomnia? Whatever your answer, you need to make allowances for that during the day. If you get up in the middle of the night, you will be more tired during the day. If possible, try to set aside some time in your daily routine for a nap. The emotional and spiritual work of re-entry takes a toll on our physical bodies. You may need more rest than usual.
_____
_____
_____

Is there one thing you would do differently? For instance, you could listen to calming music or use some essential oils before bed.
_____

How is your nutrition?

How would you explain your current eating habits, overall?
_____
_____

On an average day of eating, what would a typical day look like?

Breakfast:

Snack:

Lunch:

Snack:

Dinner:

Snack:

How much water are you consuming daily? _____

Does anything come to mind that you would like to change regarding your nutrition? If so, choose one idea.
_____
_____
_____
_____

How is your physical movement?

Are you doing any type of physical movement? Going for a walk, doing strength exercises, and even yardwork and housework chores are all types of movement. There isn't one that is better than the other.

_____
_____
_____
_____
_____
_____
_____

Is there anything you would like to do differently or add to your daily routine regarding physical movement? You can start off slowly.

_____
_____
_____
_____
_____

Now choose **only one** that you will implement during your time in *Restore*.

_____
_____
_____
_____

Here are a few pointers to keep in mind as you decide:

If you need to make a sleep and nutrition change, change nutrition first.
You have more control over what you eat than how you sleep.

If you want to start an exercise routine, start off slowly, like a *Couch to 5K* running program or a *7-minute High-Intensity Interval Training (HIIT)* workout.

Nourish Your Heart Through Input

Emotional trauma can cause a heart wound. In re-entry, this can happen when multiple experiences pile on top of each other. We will get more in-depth on that subject later. For now, we need to keep our hearts as open as possible, and you need to be receiving more heart input than output. An easy way to protect your heart is by listening to uplifting worship music, a fun audiobook, or an interesting podcast. This doesn't necessarily need to be spiritual, but it needs to be uplifting, encouraging, and fun.

What are ways you are nourishing your heart?

_____
_____
_____
_____

In what ways would you like to nourish your heart?

_____
_____
_____

Here are a few pointers to keep in mind as you decide how you want to nourish your heart:

Your heart is where you connect with God.
Your heart is the wellspring of life.

Now think about how you would like to nourish it during your time in *Restore*.

_____
_____
_____
_____

Nourish Your Soul Through Prayer and Rest

How is your prayer life?

During *Restore*, it can be hard to keep a regular Bible study routine. There are definitely seasons for that practice, but it's OK if it is not right now. Remember that prayer is a conversation. Remember, too, that you have the Psalm 23 prayer that you can cling to during your time in *Restore*.

Maintain a posture of non-judgment as you answer the following question.

What does your prayer life look like right now? Would you consider it pretty good or non-existent?
(Remember, there is no right or wrong answer.)

_____
_____
_____
_____
_____
_____
_____
_____
_____
_____

Would you be interested in trying out a new spiritual practice? See Recommended Resources for some ideas.

_____
_____
_____
_____
_____
_____
_____
_____
_____
_____

How are you resting?

When we think of the word rest, we usually think that it means sleep. In reality, rest can be so much more.

Did you know that you can Actively Rest? Here are some examples.

Physical: Plant a garden or organize the house
Creative: Draw, paint, sculpt, or color in adult coloring books
Spiritual: Spend time in God's word
Emotional: Watch a movie
Social: Get a cup of coffee with a friend
Investigative: Research something through various methods (my favorite)

These activities can invigorate even more than an afternoon nap. However, if you need to take a nap, then, by all means, take one!

Which one would you like to implement during *Restore*?
Draw a picture below or journal about how you would like to spend your time resting.

Here are a few pointers to keep in mind regarding your Soul

Our soul is where God meets us!
Add a simple Breath prayer you can use when you feel overwhelmed or anxious.

An example of a Psalm 23 Breath Prayer would be:
Breathe in, *"The Lord is my Shepherd."*
Breathe out, *"I lack nothing."*

Now choose only one idea that you would like to implement during *Restore*.

_____
_____
_____
_____

Reflection

Looking back on today's work, what would you like to implement, incorporate, or change to keep these areas nourished:

Body

_____
_____
_____
_____

Heart

_____
_____
_____
_____

Soul

_____
_____
_____
_____

Remember to give grace in this transition season. Share your intentions with a friend or small group.

End today by remembering your Declaration Verse.

Day 4
Building Safety

Yesterday, we looked at nourishing your body, heart, and soul. If you were unable to finish the Day 3 material, you can go back and work on it now. Once you're finished with that, we can now begin to build some physical and emotional safety.

To build safety, we need to do two things: we need to create safe places, and we also need to make sure we have safe people in our lives so we can share our hard experiences with them. We will start with safe places. You'll figure out where your safe places are, and you'll set up specific times to be in those places.

Safe Places

Think through your typical day. Where do you feel physically and emotionally safe? Is it at home or somewhere else, like a coffee shop with headphones or a cabin in the woods? Write down a few of your safe places.

_____ , _____ , _____
_____
_____

Can you visit any of these places daily? If not, where might you go on a daily basis to feel safe?

Please be as specific as possible:
_____
_____

Specific Time

Think through the next few months. What time of day would work best for you? (Ideally, it would be a 1- to 2-hour time frame.)

Perhaps it's early in the morning, late in the evening, or during the kids' nap time. Remember that it doesn't have to be every day, but do try to make a commitment for the next few months.)

Write down the time: _____

Safe People

Who are your safe people? These people should be good listeners, and they need to be accessible to you. They don't have to have the solution to your problem; they need to make you feel safe.

Write their names here:
_____ , _____, _____

Below fill out an accountability statement that will help you remember your takeaways from these past few days.

> I would like to spend (amount of time) _____
> working through *Restore* season in my (safe place) _____.
> I am going to be accountable to (safe person) _____
> as I create my Re-entry Path.
>
> If I can't make it to my safe place as scheduled, I will **not feel guilty.** I will give myself grace and try again tomorrow.

Pause to thank Jesus for the safe places and safe people in your life. ***End today by remembering your Declaration Verse.***

_____
_____
_____
_____
_____
_____
_____
_____
_____

Day 5
End of Week Reflection

Go back through this week's exercises. Are there any themes or anything that surprised you about what you wrote?

_____
_____
_____
_____

On Day 2, you went through an exercise that explored where you were on your Re-entry Path.

Are there any themes you saw, or was there anything that surprised you about what you wrote or processed?

_____
_____
_____
_____

How did you rest in God this week?

_____
_____
_____

Has anything else come to mind?

_____
_____
_____
_____
_____
_____
_____

Check-in for Week 1

One a scale of 1-5, which number do you connect with right now?

1   These exercises made me even more overwhelmed and hopeless. I am not ready to move on, and I need to talk to a professional counselor.

2   There is still a lot of unclarity, but I feel better about knowing there are processes I can follow. I am going to take the *Restore* season one day at a time.

3   These exercises helped me figure out a few things, and I am ready to move forward.

4   I have worked on exercises like these in another season of my life, but there are new experiences I need to work through. I am ready to move forward.

5   I couldn't come up with a single thing I need to work through; I am ready to move on to *Receive* workbook.

If you marked 1, reach out to your safe person and share your thoughts with them. If you marked any other number (including 5), then head into Week 2, and we will dig deeper into grief and loss.

You might not have finished everything for this week. You can take the weekend and work on it some more. I have seen people take a whole month to do this week's work, so please take your time to process everything. There's no rush. For the rest of today, and over the weekend, spend time listening to your favorite worship music or finding a new way to rest from Day 3.

End today by remembering your Declaration Verse.

Optional Practices for Week 1: Listening to Your Body

Carrying the hurt or anger of an offense leads the body to release stress hormones such as adrenaline and cortisol. Eliminating the perpetual flow of those hormones may also explain why forgiveness provides physical health benefits, such as lowering the risk of high blood pressure and heart problems.

As much as we don't like overwhelmed feelings, when our body is in pain, that pain is trying to tell us something is wrong. Don't ignore it.

When you hear "listen to your body," you might think that it is a New Age concept. Yoga or mindfulness meditation might even come to mind. But according to 1 Corinthians 6:19-20 (NIV), *"Do you not know that your bodies are temples of the Holy Spirit, who is in you, whom you have received from God? You are not your own; you were bought at a price. Therefore honor God with your bodies."* Depending on where you served, bodywork can be triggering because of what you have experienced in Buddhist or Hindu cultures. That is why I put this exercise as an optional practice.

Daily Bodywork Activities

Activity 1: Move for at least 10 minutes. For example, take a walk.

Activity 2: Natural Body movement. You can look this up. The most natural body movement exercises are Pilates and stretching.

Activity 3: A few times during the day, put your feet on the floor and a hand over your heart and breathe.
Notice your heart rate and breathe.
Notice the top of your head and breathe.
Then feel all the way out to your hands and breathe.
Then feel all the way down to your feet and breathe.

These activities will keep your body, heart, and soul connected.

Note: Always seek a doctor's medical advice when changing up an exercise routine.

1Psychology Today Staff writer."Forgiveness". psychologytoday. https://www.psychologytoday.com/us/basics/forgiveness.

Other Self-Care Activities

These days the concept of self-care is a debate in some Christian circles. Some people think that we need to suffer for Jesus and don't approve of self-care. But self-care isn't sitting around taking baths with candles and eating Bonbons every day. Real self-care is respecting and "listening to your body" so you can serve others out of a full cup instead of an empty one. Self-care is looking out for our emotional, spiritual, and physical sides.

Take a Bath. It has been shown that a bath gets rid of toxins in the body. (I know baths are not possible for some of my readers, but when you get a chance, try it!)

Medical massages and **Chiropractic care** have been shown to release grief and trauma in our bodies.

Brainspotting Therapy. This is an integrated mind-body therapy that I have experienced and seen fantastic results from, so I trained in it myself and can offer that as part of the re-entry path. To find out more about Brainspotting therapy, go to **shonnaingram.com.**

If you are married, be aware that **sex** can either be helpful or hurtful during this time. Talk to your spouse. If sex isn't healing for you, gently remind your spouse that this is just for a season, and come up with other ideas together. If sex is healing, then do it as much as you can.

Week 2 - *Living with Loss: A Perspective Shift*

Getting Ready for Week 2

In last week's work, we looked at how to nourish your body, heart, and soul, and we created safety so you can do this work while you rest in God. Anytime you need to go back and revisit the material, you are more than welcome to do that. This week we will look at what types of loss happened because of your transition. You might not think you have lost anything, but it is essential to check to see.

Day 1 - Introduction to Grief and Loss

Day 2 - Two Models for Grief

Day 3 - Continuing to Process the Blobs of Loss (Part 1)

Day 4 - Continuing to Process the Blobs of Loss (Part 2)

Day 5 - End of Week Reflection

Day 1
Introduction to Grief and Loss

"Loss is not the enemy; not facing its existence is.... Every loss is important. It is a part of life and cannot be avoided. Losses are necessary. You grow by losing and assessing the loss. Change occurs through loss, growth occurs through loss. Life takes in a deeper meaning because of losses. The better you handle them, the healthier you will be and the more you will grow. No one said that loss was fair, but it is part of life." - *H. Norman Wright* [2]

Elizabeth's Story Through Loss

When Elizabeth came for her next session, we reviewed her past week's work, and she said that she began seeing themes and patterns that she had never seen before. Then I asked her what comes to mind when she hears the word "grief." She remembered the time her grandfather passed away. She remembered that her mind became foggy, that there were tears and a heavy sense of confusion. She even mentioned that she had physical pain.

I shared that losing a family member or friend is a very painful experience. Most people know that grief will happen when someone passes away. However, grief also happens anytime we experience a loss. We can experience losses in many areas of our lives. I asked Elizabeth to take some time and think through other areas where she has experienced loss. She had a lot of examples, from relationship hurts to unclear expectations. She started sharing about all of those.

Then I asked her what she lost because of not being able to return to the field. She took a moment to think through this idea, and what she came up with was that she was unable to attend two weddings of national friends. But the bigger loss was that she didn't have an opportunity to share in their joyous times.

She had also recently found out that her village grandfather passed away from COVID a few months ago; she lost the opportunity to grieve with his family. Then she realized that these losses led her to lose hope that she would ever see them again.

This started her down the spiral of questioning herself. If she wasn't overseas, what was she supposed to do? She paused. "Wow, I didn't even think about how those losses connected to who I thought I was. Do you think that these compounded losses might have led me to my near crisis of faith?"

---

[2] Wright, H. Norman. *Recovering from Losses in Life*. Grand Rapid, MI: Revell, 2019.

> I told her that Dr. Diane Langberg, a Christian trauma therapist, said, "Grief often profoundly impacts someone's faith. Loss and grief raise questions about God and His goodness and trustworthiness for many people."
>
> "That explains why I am frustrated with both myself and with God during this season, even though I know I shouldn't be," Elizabeth said. "It has just been so hard, and I really couldn't put a finger on it. I haven't been able to explain it to others. Now that I know this, how do I process these losses?"
>
> I responded, "I am so glad you asked, because what we are going to see is that our losses affect us more deeply than we know. But first, let's walk through a loss exercise together."

Your turn...Reflection

What losses come to mind when you think about your re-entry?

_____
_____
_____
_____
_____
_____
_____
_____
_____
_____
_____
_____
_____
_____
_____
_____

3-Langberg, Diane. *Suffering and the Heart of God: How Trauma Destroys and Christ Restores.* Greensboro, NC: New Growth Press, 2015.

Loss Exercise

What emotions come to mind when you think through your re-entry losses? Highlight the ones you have been dealing with lately.

Disorganized	Disappointment	Shame
Guilt	Fear	Confused
Searching	Numbness	Panic
Denial	Regret	Shock
Anger	Disbelief	Irritability
Loneliness	Restlessness	Self-Criticism

Source: Wolfe, Alan. "Center for Loss and Life Transition."centerforloss.com. https//www.centerforloss.com/grief.

How have you seen these emotions rooted in your re-entry loss? Be as specific as possible.

_____
_____
_____
_____
_____
_____
_____
_____
_____
_____
_____
_____
_____
_____
_____
_____
_____
_____
_____
_____
_____
_____
_____
_____
_____
_____

End today by remembering your Declaration Verse.

Day 2
Two Models for Grief

As we saw earlier, there are a lot of emotions that are tied to our losses. At this point, we might not know everything we have lost during this season, so in this section, we will spend time finding out.

Before we start today, what are you noticing since doing yesterday's exercise?

_____
_____
_____
_____
_____
_____
_____

Do any other emotions come to mind?

_____
_____
_____

Introduction to the Grief Models

I frequently work with people in the grief and loss space. Sometimes my clients will tell me about different models they have found helpful. This is great because different approaches work for different people, and I want to have multiple models for my clients to identify with.

There are many grief models in the world, and I won't be explaining all of them. I will only be presenting two models that I have seen resonate deeply with the people I work with: "Ball in the Box" and "Blobs of Loss."

Not long ago, someone recommended a grief model called "Ball in the Box." The idea behind this model is that you have one "ball of grief" that hits a trigger every once in a while. As time goes on, the "ball of grief" gets smaller and smaller and hits the trigger less often, and those loss emotions dissipate.

The Ball in the Box

(Analogy of Grief as told to Lauren Herschel by her doctor) [4]

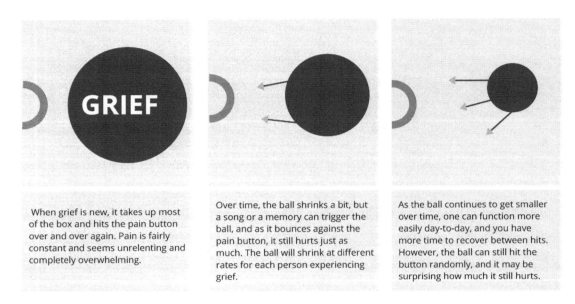

When grief is new, it takes up most of the box and hits the pain button over and over again. Pain is fairly constant and seems unrelenting and completely overwhelming.

Over time, the ball shrinks a bit, but a song or a memory can trigger the ball, and as it bounces against the pain button, it still hurts just as much. The ball will shrink at different rates for each person experiencing grief.

As the ball continues to get smaller over time, one can function more easily day-to-day, and you have more time to recover between hits. However, the ball can still hit the button randomly, and it may be surprising how much it still hurts.

Even though I connected with the "Ball in the Box" model, it didn't explain what I personally experienced or what I was seeing with my clients. The "Ball in the Box" model assumes that we are only carrying around one loss emotion or one grief at a time.

In my experience, people often carry around more than one ball of grief at a time. In real life, emotions are not a simple circular ball, and losses feel more like blobs than smooth, round balls. In my work with clients, I noticed that these blobs could come in different sizes and that each blob might not affect a person the same way.

Not only that, but these blobs were not just running into the trigger, they were running into each other. This meant that different blobs were causing different emotions on different days. The result was unstructured, potentially overwhelming feelings whose source could not be precisely pinpointed. This led me to created the Blobs of Loss model, which you can see on the next page.

[4] Schwebel, Marty. "Grief is like a ball in a box". newroadscounseling. https://newroadscounseling.com/grief-is-like-a-ball-in-a-box/Grief.

Blobs of Loss

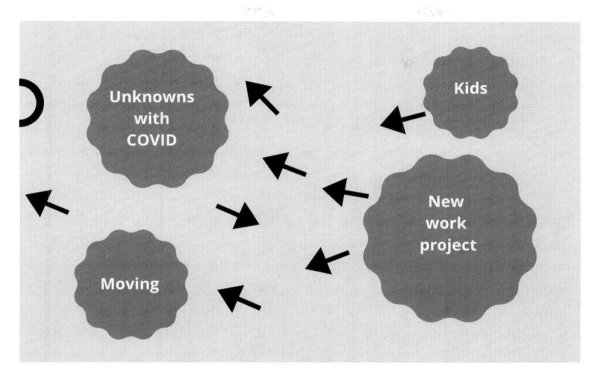

    This model seemed to more accurately reflect what I was seeing and hearing missionaries experience. A grief model like this would have helped me realize I was in trauma much earlier than I did. I would have realized that I was stuck and that I was holding on to a bunch of blobs and that I hadn't had time to grieve earlier losses. My body, heart, and soul had become disconnected from each other. Not because of one big trauma event, but a bunch of unknowns and unprocessed griefs. I couldn't explain this to anyone. It's not that I didn't want to; I just didn't know how and I couldn't explain what was happening. I tried talking to professionals, but they didn't understand why just returning home from living overseas would cause me so much unclarity.

I started using this grief model at missionary retreats, career development, and trauma groups, and it became one of my top resources. We would work through the exercise in a morning session, and then the participants would go out and spend time by themselves or in a one-on-one session with me. When they returned for the next session, they usually added three or four more blobs to their box.

Now it is your turn. You have an opportunity to work through your own "Blobs of Loss" exercise on the next page.

Your turn...Reflection

What "Blobs of Loss" are you carrying around? Be as specific as possible and take your time. (Use the next few pages to expand and process.)

My Blobs of Loss

Use the next few pages to expand on your blobs.

_____
_____
_____
_____
_____
_____
_____
_____

If needed, add more Blobs.

End today by remembering your Declaration Verse.

Day 3
Continuing to Process the Blobs of Loss (Part 1)

Now that you have taken a break, take a moment and ask Jesus if there are any other "Blobs of Loss" that need to be added to Day 2.

_____
_____
_____

Processing Your "Blobs of Loss"

Return to your "Blobs of Loss" exercise. Using the columns below, think through each blob. Ask yourself, **"Can I control anything going on in this loss?"** For example, if you haven't felt physically well for a while, and you have a choice to call the doctor or put it off, that is something you can control.

However, there are times when **we cannot control anything,** but the loss still affects us. A family member's health issue is an example of this. You could also be facing a situation where something is affecting you, but you just **don't have the energy to deal with it today.**

Continue processing your "Blob of Loss 1"

What I can control in this loss	**What I cannot control in this loss**	**This loss is affecting me, but I don't have the emotional energy right now**

Continue processing your "Blob of Loss 2"

I can control	I cannot control	Not now

Continue processing your "Blob of Loss 3"

I can control	I cannot control	Not now

As you process your Blobs, take note that the columns are fluid and will change over time.

_____
_____
_____
_____
_____
_____

Close out your time with a quick prayer, and give over to Jesus what you can today.

A prayer for this might be:

Dear Jesus, as I look over these blobs today, I thank you for allowing me to see what I can and cannot control. I give myself over to You, to start the healing process in me. Lead me by the still waters.

End today by remembering your Declaration Verse.

Day 4
Continuing to Process the Blobs of Loss (Part 2)

Today, we will use the information we collected from Day 3 and do an exercise for all the columns. The first is "**What I can control**."
The goal for this exercise is to come up with an action plan.

Ask yourself:
What can I do in this situation next week, month, year?

What is the next step you can take to help lead to a preferred outcome for Blob 1?

Next Week:

Next Month:

Next Year:

What about Blob 2?

Next Week:

Next Month:

Next Year:

What about Blob 3?

Next Week:

Next Month:

Next Year:

"What You Can't Control" Column
Release Exercise

For the Blobs that you have no control over, when you are ready, set aside some time and release them into His care. There are many different release exercises you can do. It could be as simple as writing down each blob on separate sheets of paper and throwing them away or going on a walk in nature and tearing them up as you walk along and throwing them in waste containers along the way. In retreat settings or in a small group we have burned them or written them on small rocks and thrown them into a lake. All of these release exercises allow Jesus into this space and show that you trust Him.

As you do this exercise, you might say something like:

Jesus, I release this loss to you. This doesn't mean that I am forgetting it. I simply ask you to carry it for me.

Which Release exercise comes to mind? When, where, and how are you going to do it?
_____
_____
_____

"Not Now" Column
Envelope Exercise

If there are multiple blobs that you don't have the emotional capacity to work on right now, write them down individually on sheets of paper and put them in an envelope. Put the envelope in a safe place.
This practice allows you to release space in your mind and heart while knowing these things are still a concern for you. Mark a time on your calendar to look at them again, perhaps a month from now, perhaps six months from now. As you may still be working through the re-entry workbooks at that time, I will remind you to take a look at your envelope at different times during the series.

Which blobs would you like to put into an envelope to save for later?
_____
_____

These exercises can be used long after your Re-entry Path is over to reflect on your life.

End today by remembering your Declaration Verse.

Day 5
End of Week Reflection

I know that this week might have brought up a lot of emotions, as well as some new things you realize you need to process. As I mentioned earlier, the Blobs of Loss is a tool you can continue to use to process deeper layers of loss, and you can always come back to it. Today we are going to sit with what you have already done.

Are there any themes you saw, or was there anything that surprised you about what you wrote or processed?

_____
_____
_____
_____

With whom would like you to share this?

_____
_____

Has your perspective of loss changed this week?

_____
_____

How did you rest in God this week?

_____
_____
_____

Write out your reflection on what you learned this week. (You will need this for the reflection exercises in Week 6.)

_____
_____
_____
_____

End today by remembering your Declaration Verse. Over the weekend you can finish up this week (if you haven't) and spend some time restoring your body, heart, and soul by putting on some worship music or choosing a new rest idea from Week 1. If you like to journal, you can use the next page.

*If you need an extra "Blob of Loss" worksheet, you can download it for free at **https://shonnaingram.com/product/grief-perspective-change**. Simply enter the coupon code "free."*

Extra space to journal and pray through what you have learned this week.

Week 3 - *Practice of Lament: Our Heart's Cry*

Getting Ready for Week 3

So far on the Re-entry Path, we have started grieving your losses and found new ways to rest. Today you will be introduced to another tool you can use in the grieving process called a Lament, which means to express grief, sorrow, or regret. Even though you were introduced to a quick Release exercise last week, this week we will learn that making a Lament is a practice you can use as you continue on your re-entry path.

Day 1 - Introduction to the Practice of Lament

Day 2 - Three Parts of a Lament

Day 3 - Spend Time in a Biblical Lament

Day 4 - Write Your Lament

Day 5 - End of Week Reflection

Day 1
Introduction to the Practice of Lament

"Lament is not our final prayer. It is a prayer in the meantime. Most of the lament psalms end with a 'vow to praise'—a promise to return thanksgiving to God for His deliverance. Because Jesus Christ is risen from the dead, we know that sorrow is not how the story ends. The song may be in a minor motif now, but one day it will resolve in a major chord. When every tear is wiped away, when death is swallowed up in victory, when heaven and earth are made new and joined as one, when the saints rise in glorious bodies...then we will sing at last a great, 'Hallelujah!' For now, we lift our lament to God as we wait with hope. Even so, come, Lord Jesus." - N.T. Wright [5]

Elizabeth's Laments

At our next session, we debriefed the Blobs of Loss grief tool. Elizabeth realized that there were some really deep wounds from her past that she needed to work through. It took her about a week to work through the grieving tool, but in the end, she made a few plans about the things she could and couldn't control, which meant that she was ready for the next tool: The Practice of Lament.

I started that day's conversation by asking her if she had ever heard of Laments?

"Maybe," she replied. "Something they did in the Old Testament, something Job did, and I think we study about laments in the Psalms?"

"A lament is an expression of pain, grief, and struggle," I responded. "It is a time to be honest with your feelings. It is where we ask God about 'Why?' (Why did this happen?) or 'How?' (How long, oh Lord?). Some people might have lamented in a journal entry here and there, but the practice of lament involves crying out to our Abba Father when we can't see what comes next. It expresses sorrow, it shows regret, and it is very Biblical. It is a way to connect our head and heart, and it changes our soul."

---

[5] Wright, N.T. "Five things to know about lament". ntwrightonline. https://www.ntwrightonline.org/five-things-to-know-about-lament.

There are many examples of laments in the Bible. In fact, 70 percent of the Psalms are laments, including Psalm 23 that we have been using throughout *Restore*. There is even a whole book of the Bible called Lamentations.

Descriptions of lament include crying uncontrollably, expressing great sorrow, and showing regret and disappointment. I've found that the practice of lament gives us space to express our grief to God. When we lament, we let go of our grief in a deeper way, and we need to do that before we can move on to the next step, which is forgiveness.

For me personally, learning how to practice lament was how God met me and how I began my healing and re-entry process. Lament is my most requested workshop or retreat topic, and I have walked many people through this practice. What I have found is that for those in their re-entry season, most laments are about disappointments and regret. In times like these, it is good to remember that God knows us and that He doesn't reject us in our human state. In my experience, American culture does not practice lament on a regular basis. This is unfortunate because lament is both healthy and God-honoring.

As you think through the definition of lament, how have you seen it expressed?

_____
_____
_____
_____
_____
_____
_____

What has been your experience with laments?

_____
_____
_____
_____
_____
_____
_____
_____

End today by remembering your Declaration Verse.

Day 2
Three Parts of a Lament

On Day 1, we looked at the different ways we have seen the Practice of Lament. Today, we will look at a few different parts of a lament.

There are normally seven segments to a Biblical lament. We will spend our time focusing on only three sections of a lament.

Remember whom you are talking to.
Express your honest feelings.
Vow to trust.

Remember whom you are talking to:

We are talking to the creator of the universe! He knows the number of hairs on your head. He wants what is best for you. He is your strength and shield.

Express your honest feelings:

This includes your complaints, struggles, anger, and pain, and **it is the only part of the lament that is required.** Did a situation not get resolved the way you wanted or expected? Did God not fix the situation the way you thought He should? Did an expectation not get met? Tell Him about it.

Vow to trust:

We don't need to end every lament with a **Vow to Trust**, as not every psalm of lament ends that way (see Psalm 88). However, I think we can always find something to thank God for, even if it has nothing to do with our complaints. For example, we can praise God that the sun came out today, or we can vow to trust Him in this season. Consider ending your lament in this way.

Extra: Ask Boldly [6]

In his book *Dark Clouds, Deep Mercy*, author Mark Vroegop added a fourth element: **Ask Boldly.** If you are in a place where you would like to add this to your lament, I would recommend that as well.

---

[6] Vroegop, Mark. *Dark Clouds, Deep Mercy, Discovering the Grace of Lament.* Wheaton, IL: Crossway, 2019.

Journal and pray through what you have learned about laments.

_____

End today by remembering your Declaration Verse. Now that you have been saying your Declaration Verse daily for the past few weeks, what are you noticing inside your body, heart, and soul when you say it?

_____

Day 3
Spend Time in a Biblical Lament

Today we are slowly reading through Psalm 22 (NIV) or your favorite version. As you read through it, highlight words and phrases that stand out to you. Ask Jesus what it is that He wants you to know about those words.

My God, my God, why have you forsaken me? Why are you so far from saving me, so far from my cries of anguish? My God, I cry out by day, but you do not answer, by night, but I find no rest. Yet you are enthroned as the Holy One; you are the one Israel praises. In you our ancestors put their trust; they trusted and you delivered them. To you they cried out and were saved; in you they trusted and were not put to shame. But I am a worm and not a man, scorned by everyone, despised by the people. All who see me mock me; they hurl insults, shaking their heads. "He trusts in the Lord," they say, "let the Lord rescue him. Let him deliver him, since he delights in him." Yet you brought me out of the womb; you made me trust in you, even at my mother's breast. From birth I was cast on you; from my mother's womb you have been my God. Do not be far from me, for trouble is near and there is no one to help. Many bulls surround me; strong bulls of Bashan encircle me. Roaring lions that tear their prey open their mouths wide against me. I am poured out like water, and all my bones are out of joint. My heart has turned to wax; it has melted within me. My mouth is dried up like a potsherd, and my tongue sticks to the roof of my mouth; you lay me in the dust of death. Dogs surround me, a pack of villains encircles me; they pierce my hands and my feet. All my bones are on display; people stare and gloat over me. They divide my clothes among them and cast lots for my garment. But you, Lord, do not be far from me. You are my strength; come quickly to help me. Deliver me from the sword, my precious life from the power of the dogs. Rescue me from the mouth of the lions; save me from the horns of the wild oxen. I will declare your name to my people; in the assembly, I will praise you. You who fear the Lord, praise him! All you descendants of Jacob, honor him! Revere him, all you descendants of Israel! For he has not despised or scorned the suffering of the afflicted one; he has not hidden his face from him but has listened to his cry for help. From you comes the theme of my praise in the great assembly; before those who fear you, I will fulfill my vows. The poor will eat and be satisfied; those who seek the Lord will praise him— may your hearts live forever! All the ends of the earth will remember and turn to the Lord, and all the families of the nations will bow down before him, for dominion belongs to the Lord and he rules over the nations. All the rich of the earth will feast and worship; all who go down to the dust will kneel before him— those who cannot keep themselves alive. Posterity will serve him; future generations will be told about the Lord. They will proclaim his righteousness, declaring to a people yet unborn: He has done it!

Journal and pray through this lament.

What words, phrases, or thoughts stood out to you today as you read through the laments? What does God want you to know about this passage?

End today by remembering your Declaration Verse.

Day 4
Write Your Lament

Now that you have taken time to understand what a lament is and have spent time in a lament, take as much time as you need to write your own lament. (Use more paper if needed and as much time as you like.)

_____
_____
_____
_____
_____
_____
_____
_____
_____
_____
_____
_____
_____
_____
_____
_____
_____
_____
_____
_____
_____
_____
_____
_____
_____

Creative Lament ideas- draw, paint, or dance your lament. You can use the next page as extra space.

Extra Space: Draw, paint, or continue writing your lament.

Day 5
End of Week Reflection

This week we focused on the Biblical Practice of Lament. I hope that it was a meaningful time for you. I want to share another story with you. My father-in-law has been a pastor for almost 40 years, and he said that he had never practiced lament. But when I asked him to go through this workbook, he found that writing a lament was such a powerful experience that he now does it monthly.

With whom can you share your lament?
_____

Did this exercise bring up anything you need to grieve?

_____
_____
_____
_____
_____
_____
_____
_____

How did you rest in God this week?
_____
_____
_____

Write your reflections on what you learned this week. (You will need this for the reflection exercises in Week 6.)

_____
_____
_____
_____
_____

End today by remembering your Declaration Verse.
Over the weekend finish up this week if you haven't and spend some time restoring your body, heart, and soul by putting on some worship music or choosing a new rest idea from Week 1. If you like to journal, you can use the next page.

Extra space for processing Week 3.

Week 4 - ***Self-Forgiveness: Forgiveness or Release***

Getting Ready for Week 4

So far we have looked at your losses and learned about the practice of Lament. Now we can go on to the next trauma principle which is Forgiveness. Forgiveness is such a big topic that I split it up into two weeks. There are two forgiveness areas we need to work through: the first is forgiving ourselves, and the second is forgiving others. This week we will be focusing on self-forgiveness. We need to start here because, if we can receive true forgiveness for ourselves, we will know that it is a gift, and we will be better equipped to forgive others.

Day 1 - Introduction to Self-Forgiveness

Day 2 - Difference between Unhealthy Guilt and Shame

Day 3 - Lies (First Root of Unhealthy Guilt and Shame)

Day 4 - Expectations (Second Root of Unhealthy Guilt and Shame)

Day 5 - Release Exercise

Day 1
Introduction to Self-Forgiveness

If we really want to love, we must learn to forgive - *Mother Teresa*

Elizabeth's Self-Forgiveness

Elizabeth came into the office the next week and looked exhausted. "These past few weeks, I have done some really hard inner work. I am so glad we are doing this together because I don't think I could do it on my own." She added in a defeated manner, "Do we really need to talk about forgiveness today? I am not sure my brain can handle it."

I responded, "We don't have to talk about it if you aren't ready. Let's wait a week to see how you feel. Tell me, what has been going on these past few weeks?" She started telling me about a really hard situation with a family member, which led her to experience a few setbacks.

I told her that it was completely normal and that what she was working through was really hard and would take time to process. I told her I was happy she came in and was open and honest about what was going on. We prayed together, and she left.

A week later, she came to her session a little lighter and brighter. She said she slept well this past week, and she was ready to work through the next tool.

I responded, "This happens a lot. One day we'll be fine, and the next day we feel like we were run over by a bus. We are creating new neural pathways, and that takes energy. Now that you are ready, we are going to work through self-forgiveness exercises to see if forgiveness is what you need."

"What do you mean, what I need? Of course, I need forgiveness. Don't we all?" she asked curiously.

"Yes," I told her, "that is true, but there might be something deeper going on. So let's find out!"

Healthy Guilt Exercise

Growing up in Sunday School, we learned that when we feel "bad" or feel "bad about ourselves," we probably did something wrong. We, therefore, need to ask for forgiveness.

For example, think through these different lists:

10 Commandments (outward)

You shall have no other gods before Me.

You shall not make idols.

You shall not take the name of the Lord your God in vain.

Remember the Sabbath and keep it holy.

Honor your father and mother.

You shall not steal.

You shall not murder.
(even if you wish it)

You shall not commit adultery.

You shall not bear false witness against your neighbor.
(including gossip)

You shall not covet.

7 Mind Sins (inward)

Lust   Gluttony   Greed   Sloth

Wrath   Envy   Pride

How have you seen these sins play out in your life?

_____
_____
_____
_____
_____
_____

Have you ever experienced any of these sins limiting God's work in your life or holding you back from your relationship with Christ?

_____
_____
_____
_____

It is normal to feel guilty about these sins. I call this "**healthy guilt**," and it should go away after we truly repent. The feelings may not disappear immediately, but once you start the repentance process, the feelings will go away eventually.

Spend some time asking Jesus to show you any sins that you are currently holding on to based on the ten commandments and seven mind sins. (If you need more room to process, there is a processing page on the next page.)

_____
_____
_____
_____
_____

If you truly repent, remember:

You need to accept His grace and mercy

You will be tempted to do these things again

Living out your forgiveness will allow you to forgive others

Prayer:
Lord, I truly repent for _____, _____, _____. I ask for your help as I change my ways.

We will talk more about repentance in *Rebuild*, but for now, I just wanted to share about healthy guilt because tomorrow I will introduce you to **"unhealthy guilt"** and **"shame."**

Finish today thanking Jesus for dying on the cross for these sins. What a gift He has given us!

End today by remembering your Declaration Verse.

Extra space for processing Healthy Guilt

Day 2
Difference between Unhealthy Guilt and Shame

Now that we understand the role Healthy Guilt plays in our lives, we can start looking at Unhealthy Guilt and the word that I hear a lot more lately, Shame. Again, this is just a brief overview of these subjects. People spend years in therapy in these two areas. I often see these issues pop up in the lives of missionaries, especially with those who had to return home unexpectedly.

Elizabeth's Story Continued

After Elizabeth completed the *Healthy Guilt* exercise, she saw that the sin of Pride was something she needed to confess. She saw how it was hurting her relationship with her sister. She called her sister and asked for forgiveness, and in the end, she truly felt better. However, she still had a nagging feeling of guilt, and she couldn't figure out where it was coming from.

I told her that we would be working through the concept of guilt in the next section. I told her that sin is not always at the root of a feeling of guilt or shame. According to Dr. Patti Ashley, "The neurobiology of shame looks very similar to trauma in the body."

"So what you are saying is that this uncomfortable feeling might be resulting from a trauma response and not from a sin I committed?" Elizabeth asked.

"Yes. Just like anger or disappointment are secondary emotions to grief, guilt and shame can be secondary emotions to trauma," I explained.

"How do we know the difference?" she asked.

"Today, we will spend some time looking at the differences between healthy guilt, unhealthy guilt, and shame.

---

6 Ashley, Patti. "The neurobiology of Trauma and Shame". pesi. https://www.pesi.com/blog/details/1830/the-neurobiology-of-trauma-and-shame.

A quick overview of the difference between two types of guilt and shame

Healthy Guilt arises when we sin and feel guilt.
Unhealthy Guilt arises when we act against our values.
Shame arises from deeply held beliefs about our unworthiness as a person.

	Healthy Guilt	**Unhealthy Guilt**	**Shame**
[7] Defined By:	Discomfort about something I did wrong	Something I did against my unrealistic high standard	Painful feeling of being fundamentally flawed
Caused By:	Behaviors that go against my belief system	Unrealistic expectations or irrational high standards	An innate sense of being worthless or inherently defective
How to resolve:	Repair the damage I caused	Correct my belief	Correct the internalized and deeply held belief
Freedom:	Admit behavior, take responsibility, seek true forgiveness	Find and resolve the underlying root, seek connection with others	Move away from self-criticism, find and resolve the underlying root, seek connection with others

When you look at this graph, can you pinpoint any places in your life where you are dealing with "Unhealthy Guilt" or "Shame"? Has anything in your re-entry experience caused Unhealthy Guilt or Shame?

_____
_____
_____
_____

You might need more time and space to unpack what this means for you. You have an extra processing page. We will be spending the rest of this week learning about two root causes of "Unhealthy Guilt" and "Shame," but this is enough for today.

End today by remembering your Declaration Verse.

7 NICABM staff writer. "Guilt vs. Shame [Infographic]". nicabm. https://www.nicabm.com/guilt-vs-shame.

Extra space for processing Unhealthy Guilt and Shame

Day 3
Lies (First Root of Unhealthy Guilt and Shame)

There are many roots that cause guilt and shame, but for our time together, we will be examining two: **Lies** and **Expectations**.

I frequently see these two roots as I work with missionaries and especially those in a re-entry season. **It's important to spend time working through them because they block us from accepting our rights as a child of God.**

Today we will be discussing lies. We will start by looking at a list of commonly held lies that missionaries in re-entry often believe. We will be discussing why we believe them later this week.

Circle any lie that causes something to happen in your body, heart, or soul when you read it. Note: these lies might be triggering. If they are, you can spend some time talking to Jesus about them.

Common Lies People in Re-entry Believe

I am not doing enough	**I am broken**
Vulnerability is weakness	**I can do it on my own**
I need to perform to be seen	**I am alone**

I will be the first to admit that I believed some of these lies during my re-entry season. As I read them today, my internal response is to notice that, while I used to believe them, I have received healing from them.

Which ones did you circle? Which ones were you surprised by?
There is extra processing space on the next page.

_____
_____
_____

Extra space for processing lies I believe

_ If you need to stop here for today, you can reach out to someone you trust and spend some time working through this.

Where do these lies come from?

Lies we believe come from many different sources. I know we have all heard that lies come from Satan, as he is the Father of lies. It would be better if he just came out with the lies so we would know what they are; instead, he uses half-truths and even uses people we love.

I believe that most Christians have good intentions. But sometimes people say things that affect our beliefs about who we are as a child of God. An example of this happened just the other day. I was talking with a field leader who was told by his director that his job was to "make all sides happy." This could not be done. This made the field leader feel deep shame and unhealthy guilt from his director because he couldn't do what he was told to do. I am sure the director was not trying to make the team leader feel guilty. The director was probably just frustrated with the situation.

You can begin figuring out where lies come from in your life by looking at the following areas:

Family of Origin
Have you heard, "You should be more like…"?

Culture (teachers, social media, etc.)
Have you heard, "You aren't pretty/good/smart enough"? This leads us to compare ourselves to the world's standards.

Your Own Mind
Have you ever thought, "I am not good enough because I don't have_____"?

Specific to Missions
Church missions team, missions organization, or teammates ever told you something that you started believing was true?

Reflection

What lies are you believing during your re-entry season?

_____
_____
_____
_____
_____
_____
_____
_____
_____
_____
_____
_____
_____
_____
_____

We will process these lies at the end of the week. For now, we are just naming them. You can use the envelope exercise from the first week if needed. I know that this can be hard emotional work, and you might feel stuck here for a few days. Just know that you aren't alone and if you are feeling overwhelmed, you can put the book down for a few days.

My prayer is that you don't leave today upset or overwhelmed. Think of it as a blessing that we had an opportunity to unearth these lies and that we don't have to believe them anymore.

End today by remembering your Declaration Verse.
Spend time in worship music and out in nature if possible. We will be here when you are ready to move to the next step and talk about expectations.

Extra space for journaling and talking to Jesus about the lies

Day 4
Expectations (Second Root of Unhealthy Guilt and Shame)

The sister root of lies is expectations, especially unrealistic or unmet expectations. I see this playing out even more than lies among those in a transition season. The best book I ever read on the subject was *Expectations and Burnout: Women Surviving the Great Commission.*[8]

Elizabeth's Expectation

If you remember from the beginning of Elizabeth's story, she came in to see me because she was burned out. Here is why.

Growing up, Elizabeth was a good student who liked school. She excelled at learning languages. When she was seven years old, her mom told her, "You are just like my Aunt Mary who was a Bible Translator. She was such a servant of God!" When Elizabeth started college, her New Testament professor told her she had a gift for languages. While she could do the work, she didn't find translation all that fulfilling, and there were many areas of the translation process that were difficult for her. She had various health issues before heading overseas, but she thought that her health issues would go away if she went overseas. She believed that if God called her to it, then He would get her through it. Besides, wasn't she doing what **God wanted her to do?** In her head at the time, it all made sense.

Once Elizabeth arrived on the field, her health almost immediately declined, which led to bouts of depression. She felt like she was failing herself, God, and her parents' dream for her.

During our time together, Elizabeth realized that she had put some expectations on herself and that some of those expectations were unrealistic. She knew that going to a developing country would likely make her health decline, but instead, she thought that if she just had enough faith, it would all work out. She also realized that she was placing her identity in what she **could do for God** rather than allowing Him to work through her.

Where Do Unrealistic and Unmet Expectations Come From?

My definition of an unrealistic expectation is a strong belief that we are supposed to do or be something we don't need to do or be (at least in that season of our lives).

---

8 Eenigenburg, Sue. *Expectations And Burnout: Women Surviving the Great Commission.* Pasadena, CA: William Cary Library. 2010.

For example, deep down Elizabeth was trying to be her Aunt Mary. Even though no one was telling her she should be, she put that expectation on herself. When she couldn't live up to what she thought she should be doing, she felt like it was her fault and that she was broken. Unmet expectations are those expectations we put on other people that they don't or can't meet. For example, when you expect something from a family member and your expectation wasn't communicated well and they didn't meet it.

What are some Unrealistic or Unmet Expectations you have experienced in your re-entry season?

During a re-entry season, I have seen unrealistic or unmet expectations come from

Sending Churches
Sending Organization
On-field and Off-field Teammates
Family or Friends

Do you have any unrealistic or unmet expectations about your re-entry?

Sending Church or Missions Team

_____
_____

Sending Organization

_____
_____

On-field and Off-field field teammates

_____
_____

Family or Friends

_____
_____
_____

Like yesterday, my prayer is that you don't leave today upset or overwhelmed. Think of it as a blessing that we had an opportunity to unearth these expectations and that we don't have to believe them anymore.

End today by remembering your Declaration Verse.

Extra space for journaling and talking to Jesus about unrealistic or unmet expectations.

Day 5
Release Exercise

You made it to the end of this week! You might have taken more than a week to process all of this, but I hope you got started because this is something you can use beyond the re-entry season.

You might be asking how **lies** and **expectations** relate to this week's topic of **self-forgiveness**. Well, in order to forgive, we need to release the resentment or anger we have toward ourselves, and to do this, we must release the hold the lies or expectations have on us.

Release Exercise

To be free from these lies and expectations, you can take the opportunity to release them to Jesus. Then spend some time asking Jesus what He wants you to know about these lies.

Choose one of the lies and expectations you would like to **renounce** and **release.**

Pray this out loud: *Jesus, there are many lies that I need you to take away today. I choose to renounce and release the lies of _____. I choose to renounce and release the expectation of _____.*

Once we release the lies and expectations we have been believing, we might feel a hole in our spirit. We need to fill that hole with the truth of who we are in Christ. We need to replace lies and expectations with the truth.

Receiving Freedom from these Lies and Expectations[9]

Declare one or two of these out loud daily.

I am washed, sanctified, and justified by the blood of Jesus (1 Cor 6:11)
I am regenerated and renewed by the Holy Spirit (Titus 3:5)
I am born again into a living hope (1 Peter 1:3)
I am a child of God (John 1:12)
I am one with God the Father and Jesus the Son (John 17:25)
I am alive to God in Christ Jesus (Rom 6:11)
I am an heir of God, a joint heir with Christ (Rom 8:17)

---

9 Reasons for Hope* Jesus."101 Truths about our identity in Christ." reasonsforhopejesus. https://reasonsforhopejesus.com /101-truths-identity-in-christ.

End of Week Reflection

This week we started the process of unpacking some deeply held beliefs, lies, and expectations. This is hard work, so go out and celebrate! If you remember at the beginning of our time together, I mentioned that Restoration is a continuous process. So don't grow weary: you can continue being restored!

Things to remember:

Take a breath and praise Him for release

You might need another round of the "Blobs of Loss" exercise or to spend some time to lament

Take as much time as needed

Go out and do something fun

Spend time at the still waters

Receive grace in the process

Did this exercise bring up anything you need to grieve?

_____
_____
_____
_____

How did you rest in God this week?

_____
_____
_____

What are some of your reflections from this week's work? (You will need this for the Week 6 review page.)

_____
_____
_____
_____

To those who deal with lies and unrealistic expectations, my heart is with you. I pray that you have a good friend, coach, or therapist to continue to walk you through this process. If you don't, I would love to connect with you as you continue to Rest in God.

Extra space for journaling

Week 5 - *Forgiving Others: Covenant Promise*

Getting Ready for Week 5

Last week our focus was on forgiving yourself. Forgiving yourself is a very important step in forgiving others because we can only forgive others out of a healthy place. This week we are going to work through forgiving others.

Day 1 - Forgiving Others: It's Complicated

Day 2 - Three Levels of Forgiveness

Day 3 - Starting Your Forgiveness Journey

Day 4 - Forgiveness Exercise

Day 5 - End of Week Reflection

Day 1
Forgiving Others: It's Complicated

"Forgiveness is not an emotion, but a covenant promise to forgive the debt of your offender. Ideally, it should not be granted at the end of the healing process, but at the beginning. It is the foundation upon which relational and emotional healing may take place." - *Dr. Jeremy Lelek*

I have been teaching about forgiveness for quite a few years, and in that time I've observed some deep misunderstandings about what forgiveness is.
To help us understand the concept of Forgiveness, it is easier to start off by talking about what "Forgiveness is not."

Forgiveness is NOT:

Forgetting what happened
Letting them get away with what they did or hurt someone else again
Waiting for the offender to change their behavior
Trying to make sense of the other person's behavior

When you think about what forgiveness is not, what comes to mind?

_____
_____
_____
_____
_____
_____
_____
_____
_____
_____
_____
_____

---

10 Lelek, Jeremy. "Common myths about forgiveness". careleader. https://www.careleader.org/common-myths-forgiveness.

Day 2
Three Levels of Forgiveness

When I was researching forgiveness, I came across Dr. Stephen Marmer's work. He is a psychiatrist at UCLA who explains forgiveness by breaking it down into three levels. Forgiveness has to do with restoring relationships, and there are three levels to mending relationships. These levels are **Exoneration, Forbearance,** and **Release**. Let's unpack these ideas further.

Exoneration

Exoneration means that the slate is completely wiped clean and that the relationship is fully restored to its previous sense of innocence. This should happen when the event was an accident for which no fault or blame can be applied. The next is when the person who committed the offense is a child or someone who wasn't capable of understanding the implications of their actions. Exoneration can also happen when the person who hurt you is truly sorry and takes full responsibility for their actions. This is what most Christians expect to happen, even in incidents that might need another step or two for this to happen. So, let's take a look at the second level called Forbearance.

Forbearance

The second level of forgiveness gets a little more complicated. According to Dr. Marmer, Forbearance is when an offender either makes a partial apology or they are only partially to blame for their wrong behavior. While an apology may be offered, it usually doesn't fix the issue or may feel inauthentic. (The often-heard, "I'm sorry you feel that way" or "If I did anything to upset you, I'm sorry" come to mind.)

Forbearance comes into play when the relationship at hand is important to you. However, unlike exoneration, with forbearance there is a loss of trust. It is recommended that the person offering forgiveness maintain a degree of watchfulness. This is similar to "forgive but don't forget" or "trust but verify."

With forbearance, you're able to continue relationships with people who are important to you but who may not be fully trustworthy, at least at the present time. Maybe in the future, there can be Exoneration.

From a Christian perspective, forbearance is a fruit of the spirit otherwise known as patience. I believe that there are things we can't do on our own, and forbearance forgiveness is one of them. We need to allow Jesus to help us do this.

11 Marmer, Stephen. "3 types of forgiveness". aish. https://www.aish.com/three-types-of-forgiveness.

Release

Release applies to situations in which the person who hurt you has never acknowledged any wrongdoing. They have never apologized or offered incomplete or insincere apologies. These are situations where atonement might never be made.

Some examples of where release might be the only option include:
Survivors of child abuse
Businesspeople being cheated by partners
Betrayal by friends or relatives

With Release, you don't continue the relationship. This allows you to stop defining your life by the hurt done to you. It allows you to let go and heal your heart, body, and mind when there doesn't seem to be any way around the injury. It allows you to stop re-experiencing your traumatic past so that you can move forward.

I hope Dr. Marmer's levels of forgiveness have put words to some circumstances you experienced. But more than that, I hope you will experience Jesus as the ultimate healer of your wounds.

As you consider these levels of forgiveness, what names and situations come to mind?

Exoneration

_____
_____
_____
_____

Forbearance

_____
_____
_____
_____

Release

_____
_____
_____
_____

There is an extra processing page if you need more room. Tomorrow we will find out what to do with these names.

End today by remembering your Declaration Verse.

Who and what do you need to forgive?

Day 3
Starting your Forgiveness Journey

"Forgiveness is not just about saying the words. It is an active process in which you make a conscious decision to let go of negative feelings whether the person deserves it or not..." *Karen Swartz, M.D.*

So far, we have learned what forgiveness isn't and what the different levels of forgiveness are. We've discerned whom we need to forgive and for what. Now it's time to move forward in the forgiveness process.

Forgiveness is an active process and is unclear at times, and we need to take it one day at a time. One of the pictures I use often when talking about Forgiveness is a bird leaving its cage. It is usually not a straight path.

Here are some truths to remember:
Forgiveness is a process.
Forgiveness allows us to release resentment, anger, and blame.
Forgiveness is a choice.
Forgiveness is an opportunity to release the power that person has over your life.

How does this help you on your Forgiveness Journey?

_____
_____
_____
_____
_____

End today by remembering your Declaration Verse.
If this exercise brings out emotions of loss and grief, or if you need extra time to lament, spend time doing those activities before moving to the next day's work.

12-Swartz, Karen. "Forgiveness your health depends on it. hopkinsmedicine. https://www.hopkinsmedicine.org/health/wellness-and-prevention/forgiveness-your-health-depends-on-it.
13-Hill, Harriet. *Healing the Wounds of Trauma, How the Church Can Help.* Philadelphia, PA: Trauma Healing Institute, 2020.

How does this help you on your Forgiveness Journey?

Day 4
Forgiveness Exercise

Today we get to bring to Jesus the people and situations from the list of names and [14] situations you have collected this week. I adapted this from Adele Calhoun's exercise. (It might be easier to have someone read this to you or to record the instructions for playback.)

First, find a quiet place and time with limited distractions. The next page is open for you to write out any notes you would like.

Put your hand on your heart.
"Dear Jesus, thank you for the covenant promise of forgiveness. It is because of what you did on the cross that I can receive this and give it to others."

Ask Jesus,
"What name or situation are you asking me to forgive?"

Lift your eyes to Jesus.
"What do you want me to do with these hurts and emotions? What do I need to offer in this situation? Exoneration, forbearance, or release?"

Notice how you are feeling in your heart, head, and body.
Say out loud what you are going to offer in as much detail as possible.

Place your hands on your heart.
Ask Jesus, "What wrongs have I done where I need to receive your forgiveness?"

Offer your Heart and Hands to Jesus out loud.
Say, "Jesus, I receive your forgiveness so I can do your work. I pray that you will dissolve my shame and guilt or any other emotion that is not from you. I receive your gift of freedom as a true child of God."

Then ask, "How do you want me to take this gift of forgiveness into my world and into my relationships?"

Stay there at the foot of the cross.
Spend as much time as you need.

---

14 Calhoun, Adele. *Invitations from God: Accepting God's Offer to Rest, Weep, Forgive, Wait, Remember and More.* Downers Grove, IL: IVP Press, 2011

Extra space for processing Forgiveness Exercise

Day 5
End of Week Reflection

I know this week might have been hard, but it is so needed for your Re-entry Path. Thank you for sticking with me!

How did you rest in God this week?

_____
_____
_____
_____
_____
_____
_____
_____
_____
_____
_____

Write down a few reflections from this week. (You will need this for Week 6.)

_____
_____
_____
_____
_____
_____
_____
_____
_____
_____
_____
_____

End today by remembering your Declaration Verse.

Extra space for Week 5 Notes

Optional Practice for Week 5-Deeper Listening Prayer
(*interactive prayer model*)

Christian psychiatrist Dr. Karl Lehman says that Immanuel Prayer *"Permanently rewires* [15] *traumatic memories by building an interactive connection with the living Presence of Jesus."* He believed it so much that he developed his own prayer practice, and several years ago I was trained in it.

I have been using a form of the Immanuel Prayer model on and off for the past twelve years or so. During that time I have seen the importance of combining it with daily prayer practices. Now I call it Deeper Listening Prayer.

I have already introduced you to the daily prayer practice of Psalm 23 and the breath prayers.

But sometimes we need to set a specific time to listen to Jesus. During this time we need others to walk with us as we discern what Jesus has to say.

Reasons to Engage in Deeper Listening Prayer

It allows us time and space to be aware of God's presence.
It helps us to be open to receiving His love, correction, and guidance.
It quiets our souls and minds so we can be attentive to His teaching.
It allows us to be humble toward God's Word so we can learn.
It helps us recognize our dependence on God.

There are many different training approaches for a one-on-one prayer session. My advice is to work with someone you trust and who is trained in an approach you are comfortable with. As healing as Immanuel Prayer can be, it can also be a place where spiritual manipulation can happen. To prevent this, I recommend having two prayer ministers walk with you, preferably of the same gender.

If you don't personally know anyone involved in this type of ministry, you do now. I would love to walk with you on your prayer journey. Please visit www.shonnaingram.com/contact to set up a prayer session with someone from my team.

---

15 Lehman, Karl. *Outsmarting Yourself: Catching Your Past Invading the Present and What to Do About It.* USA: The Joy! Books. 2011.

Week 6 - *Reflection and Review*

Getting Ready for Week 6 (our last week in *Restore*)

This week we will be reflecting on what we learned in *Restore* or taking the extra time to catch up. You might be feeling like this is redundant work. But it might have been a while since you went through some of these exercises, and right now we are building new neural pathways to get us ready for the next two workbooks. Looking back helps prepare us to look forward.

Spend this week looking back through your reflections and see how far you have already come. Then you will have time to think of how you would like to use these tools as you continue working through your re-entry season.

Day 1 - Reflection on Living with Loss

Day 2 - Reflection on Practice of Lament

Day 3 - Reflection on Self-Forgiveness

Day 4 - Reflection on Forgiving Others

Day 5 - Reflection on *Restore*

Day 1
Reflection on Living with Loss

Spend today looking back through your *Living with Loss* reflection page.
How would you like to move forward?

How will you implement this?

Daily:

Weekly:

Yearly:

End today by remembering your Declaration Verse.

Day 2
Reflection on Practice of Lament

Spend today looking back through your *Practice of Lament* reflection page.
How would you like to move forward?

How will you implement this?

Daily:

Weekly:

Yearly:

End today by remembering your Declaration Verse.

Day 3
Reflection on Self-Forgiveness

Spend today looking back through your *Self-Forgiveness* reflection page.
How would you like to move forward?

How will you implement this?

Daily:

Weekly:

Yearly:

End today by remembering your Declaration Verse.

Day 4
Reflection on Forgiving Others

Spend today looking back through your *Forgiving Others* reflection page. How would you like to move forward?

How will you implement this?

Daily:

Weekly:

Yearly:

End today by remembering your Declaration Verse.

Day 5
Reflection on *Restore*

What are some important principles you learned along the way in *Restore*?

How will you implement this?

Daily:

Weekly:

Yearly:

End today by remembering your Declaration Verse.

Congratulations, *you made it through Restore!*

Mark where you are right now:

1. I still have a lot of unclarity about what is going on with Jesus. I will commit to working through *Restore* again.

2. I learned a lot and feel healthier in my relationship with Jesus. I am debating if I need to stay in *Restore* for a while.

3. This is my first time through *Restore*. I feel comfortable and know how to implement what I have learned. I am ready to move on to *Receive*.

4. This is my second or more time through *Restore*. I now feel more comfortable implementing what I learned. I am ready to move on.

5. Other: _____

What was your number? If you scored a 3 or higher, it is time to go to *Rebuild*. If you need to stay in *Restore* for a little while longer, that is fine too.

We still will be here for you!

What is the next step you will take?

_____
_____
_____

Moving Towards *Receive*

Elizabeth Finishes Restore

Elizabeth came in for her last *Restore* session. She mentioned that she was starting to connect with Jesus in a different way.

Even though healing occurred during this Restore season, she still felt conflicted because she wasn't where she thought she should be by now. This led her to think that maybe she wasn't ready to move forward since she knew that more losses would pop up and that she still had more work to do around forgiveness.

I reminded her that this was a continuous process and that her time in *Restore* was just the start. She seemed to be okay with that answer, and she made a commitment to be ready to look at *Receive* in a few weeks. For now, she needed a break, so she started working on some creative projects that she had been putting off for a while.

What about you? Are you ready to move forward?

If you were able to start processing the questions on the previous page, or if you answered 3 or higher on the chart, then I am confident that it is time for you to move to *Receive*.

My prayer for you at the beginning of *Restore* was for you to learn how to process Loss through Laments and Forgiveness. Now you have some new processing tools that you can use as you continue life on the other side of re-entry. Before you leave, put a *Restore* check-in on your calendar for six months from now and one year from now.

I'm looking forward to seeing you in *Receive*, my favorite workbook!

Until then, Rest in God.

Appendix

Butterfly Hug
Anxiety in the Moment

The Butterfly Hug [16] is a therapeutic intervention method developed by Lucina Artigas, M.A., M.T., and Ignacio Jarero, Ed.D., Ph.D., M.T., to help relax and calm yourself in a moment of stress. It is recommended to practice this technique the first time when you are not in an anxious or distressed state.

Start off by putting your feet comfortably on the floor.

Notice your breath and heart beating. At this point, you don't need to take a deep breath, just check in to see how fast your heart is beating.

Notice any emotions or self-judgments coming up, and continue focusing on your breath.

Set a timer for 2 minutes.

Start by crossing your hands over your chest just below your collarbone.

Begin slowly tapping, alternating left and right, left and right until you come into a rhythm.

Continue tapping for 30 seconds to a few minutes.

If you need to see it being done, you can check out: https://www.youtube.com/watch?v=RQxKedYGyU8

Note: this exercise is for educational purposes only. If you are experiencing frequent anxiety or panic attacks, please seek out a therapist for further evaluation.

---

16 Kromroy, Sonja. "Butterfly hug". wildtreewellness. https://wildtreewellness.com/butterfly-hug.

References

Ashley, Patti. "The neurobiology of Trauma and Shame." pesi. https://www.pesi.com/blog/details/1830/the-neurobiology-of-trauma-and-shame.

Calhoun, Adele. *Invitations from God: Accepting God's Offer to Rest, Weep, Forgive, Wait, Remember and More.* Downers Grove, IL: IVP Press, 2011.

Eenigenburg, Sue. *Expectations And Burnout: Women Surviving the Great Commission.* Pasadena, CA: William Cary Library. 2010.

Kromroy, Sonja. "Butterfly hug". wildtreewellness. https://wildtreewellness.com/butterfly-hug.

Langberg, Diane. *Suffering and the Heart of God: How Trauma Destroys and Christ Restores.* Greensboro, NC: New Growth Press, 2015.

Lehman, Karl. *Outsmarting Yourself: Catching Your Past Invading the Present and What to Do About It.* USA: The Joy! Books. 2011.

Lelek, Jeremy. "Common myths about forgiveness". careleader. https://www.careleader.org/common-myths-forgiveness.

Marmar, Stephen. "3 types of forgiveness." aish. https://www.aish.com/three-types-of-forgiveness.

NICABM staff writer. "Guilt vs. Shame [Infographic]". NICABM. https://www.nicabm.com/guilt-vs-shame.

Psychology Today Staff writer. "Forgiveness". psychologytoday. https://www.psychologytoday.com/us/basics/forgiveness.

Reasons for Hope* Jesus staff writer". 101 Truths about our identity in Christ." Reasonsforhopejesus. https://reasonsforhopejesus.com/101-truths-identity-in-christ.

Schwebel, Marty. "Grief is like a ball in a box". newroadscounseling. https://newroadscounseling.com/grief-is-like-a-ball-in-a-box/Grief.

Swartz, Karen. "Forgiveness your health depends on it". hopkinsmedicine. https://www.hopkinsmedicine.org/health/wellness-and-prevention/forgiveness-your-health-depends-on-it.

Wolfe, Alan. "Center for Loss and Life Transition". centerforloss. https://www.centerforloss.com/grief.

Wright, H. Norman. *Recovering from Losses in Life.* Grand Rapid, MI: Revell, 2019.

Wright, N.T. "Five things to know about lament". ntwrightonline. https://www.ntwrightonline.org/five-things-to-know-about-lament/.

Vroegop, Mark. *Dark Clouds, Deep Mercy, Discovering the Grace of Lament.* Wheaton, IL: Crossway, 2019.

Recommended Resources

Breath prayer
https://www.soulshepherding.org/breath-prayers/
https://www.upperroom.org/resources/the-breath-prayer

Healing Prayer approaches
https://www.immanuelapproach.com/
https://www.transformationprayer.org/
https://elijahhouse.org/

Spiritual Practices
Sacred Rhythms: Arranging Our Lives for Spiritual Transformation by Ruth Haley Barton
Celebration of Discipline by Richard J. Foster

Health
https://www.health.harvard.edu/blog/autoimmune-disease-and-stress-is-there-a-link-2018071114230
https://arapc.com/stress-and-autoimmune-dieases/
https://www.goodtherapy.org/blog/how-trauma-affects-our-relationship-with-our-bodies-1205175
https://awarenessact.com/10-areas-stress-and-repressed-emotions-are-stored-according-to-this-psychotherapist-free resource from nica

Shame
The Soul of Shame by Dr. Curt Thompson

General Resources
Anatomy of the Soul by Dr. Curt Thompson
The Body Keeps the Score by Dr. Bessel Van der Kolk
https://www.athirstforgod.com/the-presence-project/ by Summer Gross
Shonnaingram.com
renewed-hope-approach.com

Check out other resources at shonnaingram.com/resources

Your Path of Renewed Hope series

Made in United States
Orlando, FL
04 March 2024